UP WITH LANGUAGE
NOUNS & PRONOUNS

 A Remedia Publication

Created by

Kitty Scharf
Barbara Johnson

REMEDIA PUBLICATIONS   10135 E. VIA LINDA, #D124   SCOTTSDALE, AZ 85258

TABLE OF CONTENTS

NOUN AND PRONOUN BOOK

AWARD

_____

has completed all the
noun and pronoun activities
and has done a terrific
job !

_____ _____
Teacher   Date

AWARD

TO _____

for completing the
Noun and Pronoun Book.
Congratulations !

_____ _____
Teacher   Date

NOUN & PRONOUN

NAME _____

PAGE	PERFECT SCORE	MY SCORE	PAGE	PERFECT SCORE	MY SCORE
3	36		24	26	
4	16		25	36	
5	26		26	36	
6	43		27	27	
7	36		28	28	
8	44		29	18	
9	30		30	38	
10	81		31	20	
11	67		32	42	
12	19		33	19	
13	28		34	16	
14	30		35	11	
15	58		36	12	
16	25		37	35	
17	47		38	7	
18	46		39	21	
19	41		40	15	
20	36		41	42	
21	39		42	35	
22	24		43	16	
23	19				

NOUNS

RECOGNITION

A NOUN IS A WORD USED TO NAME A <u>PERSON</u>, <u>PLACE</u>, OR <u>THING</u>. IT ANSWERS THE FOLLOWING QUESTIONS: WHO? WHERE? WHAT?

EXAMPLE: PERSON - doctor   John   sister
               PLACE - school   bank   Arizona
               THING - paper   London Bridge   radio

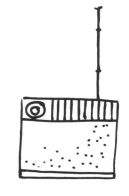

Write nouns that name persons, places, or things.

PERSON	PLACE	THING

On a separate sheet of paper, write six sentences. Use two nouns in each sentence.

NOUNS

RECOGNITION

Look for nouns in the picture.

Write the nouns that you see.

_____   _____

_____   _____

_____   _____

_____   _____

_____   _____

_____   _____

_____   _____

NOUNS

RECOGNITION

Fill in each blank with a noun.

1. Mother left some _____ on the table.

2. The two _____ nearly collided.

3. Jack threw the _____ off the bridge.

4. My father lost his _____ this morning.

5. Don hit the _____ up onto the roof.

6. Jim put _____ into his squirt gun.

7. Mary ate three _____ in five minutes.

8. I lost my _____ in the dirt.

9. Too many _____ can make you sick.

10. I yelled at my _____.

11. The _____ was covered with _____.

12. The _____ were frightened by the _____.

13. The _____ slept in the _____.

14. I like _____ and _____.

15. _____ is my favorite _____.

On a separate sheet of paper, write 6 words that name things you see in your room.

5

NOUNS

RECOGNITION

Underline the nouns in these sentences.

1. The mailman delivers letters.

2. My dad watched the game on television.

3. The dog ate the scraps in his dish.

4. Dick rode his bike to school.

5. My brother works at the bank.

6. My grandmother planted a garden.

7. Our neighbors moved to the country.

8. The farmer owns a tractor.

9. The airplane landed in Tokyo.

10. All rivers run into the sea.

Place 12 of the nouns you have underlined in the proper column.

PERSON	PLACE	THING

On a separate sheet of paper, write 8 words that name things you see around your school.

6

NOUNS

ABSTRACT AND CONCRETE

SOME NOUNS NAME THINGS YOU <u>CANNOT</u> SEE, TOUCH, SMELL, OR HEAR. SUCH NOUNS MAY NAME A FEELING OR AN IDEA.

EXAMPLES: Her <u>love</u> was strong.
              His eyes were full of <u>fear</u>.

Underline nouns you can see, touch, smell, or hear. Circle nouns that name a feeling or an idea.

1. The little dog wagged its tail with joy.

2. The teacher had high hopes for her students.

3. The boy lacked ambition and energy.

4. The man tried to hide his fear and anger.

5. The room seemed to be filled with happiness.

6. My mother planted a garden last spring.

7. My love for you is very strong.

8. The little girl needs a new coat for winter.

Place some of the nouns you have underlined or circled in the right column.

NOUNS I <u>CANNOT</u> SEE, HEAR, TOUCH, OR SMELL	NOUNS I <u>CAN</u> SEE, HEAR, TOUCH, OR SMELL
_____	_____
_____	_____
_____	_____
_____	_____
_____	_____

Choose 5 words you have circled. Use each word as a noun in a different sentence.

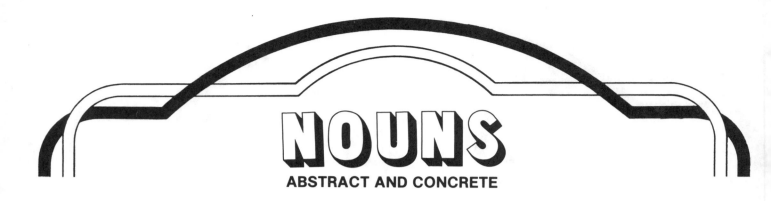

NOUNS
ABSTRACT AND CONCRETE

Underline nouns you can see, touch, smell, or hear.
Circle nouns that name a feeling or an idea.

Eskimo Boy

Paku felt happiness as he put on his gloves and parka. He turned and smiled at his mother. He had hopes of helping his father catch a walrus for dinner. His hunger for walrus was amazing. With joy, he followed his father to the sled. His father looked at him with love as he lifted the little boy onto the sled.

Killer Whale

The explorers felt fear as they spotted the killer whale. They had a desire to turn their boat around because they feared for their safety. Horror came over them as they watched the whale move toward them.

The idea of being eaten by a killer whale was frightening. With patience, they guided the boat back to shore. It takes courage to travel next to a killer whale.

Write six nouns that name a feeling or an idea.

_____ _____ _____

_____ _____ _____

On a separate sheet of paper, use each noun you have written in a different sentence.

8

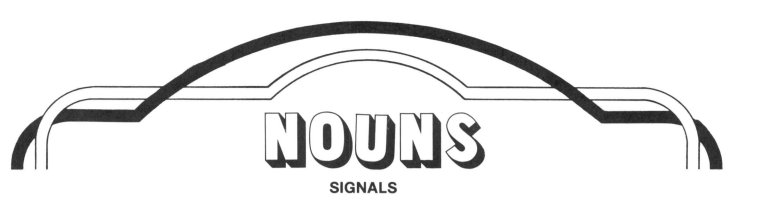

NOUNS

SIGNALS

Use <u>a</u> before:
    words that begin with consonant sounds
    words that begin with a long <u>u</u> sound

Use <u>an</u> before:
    words that begin with any vowel sound except long <u>u</u>

Write <u>a</u> or <u>an</u> before each of the following words.

1. _____ egg
2. _____ telephone
3. _____ record
4. _____ hotel
5. _____ envelope
6. _____ island
7. _____ pencil
8. _____ actress
9. _____ owl
10. _____ unit
11. _____ shelf
12. _____ elephant
13. _____ radio
14. _____ doctor
15. _____ ostrich

16. _____ antelope
17. _____ table
18. _____ eraser
19. _____ oyster
20. _____ bell
21. _____ uniform
22. _____ razor
23. _____ taxi
24. _____ umbrella
25. _____ olive
26. _____ donkey
27. _____ hero
28. _____ arrow
29. _____ grape
30. _____ parrot

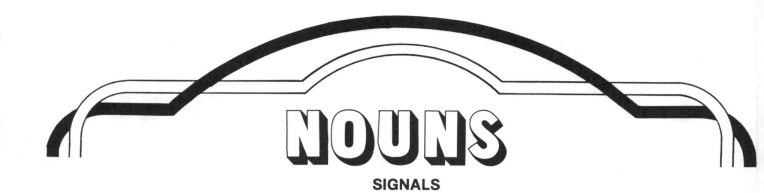

NOUNS

SIGNALS

> **A**, **AN**, AND **THE** OFTEN APPEAR BEFORE NOUNS: THEY ARE CALLED NOUN SIGNALS. EVERY TIME YOU SEE ONE, YOU KNOW A NOUN WILL FOLLOW.

Circle each noun signal in the sentences below. Underline each noun.

1. The car ran over the curb.
2. A noise woke the baby.
3. We saw an elephant at the zoo.
4. Did you put the milk in the refrigerator?
5. I found a wallet on the street.
6. The girl ate an egg for breakfast.
7. The man bought a cane.
8. The man had a beard.
9. A puppy ran across the street.
10. A mouse was caught in the trap.
11. We rode a bus home after the movie.
12. A book fell off the desk.
13. I'll pick up the children in an hour.
14. The dishes are in the cupboard.
15. An owl is sitting in a tree.
16. The secretary put the letter in an envelope.
17. Did the lady win a prize?
18. A box tumbled from the shelf.

On a separate sheet of paper, use each of the following noun signals in a different sentence: these, those, their, every, each.

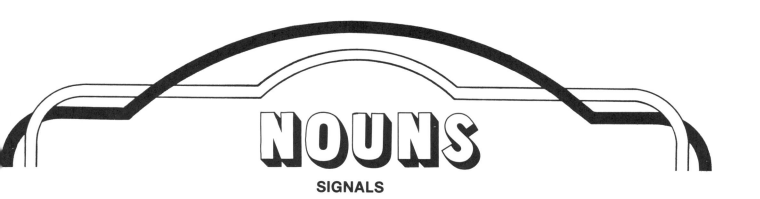

NOUNS

SIGNALS

A, AN, THE, ITS, YOUR, EVERY, THOSE, EACH, THEIR, OUR, THAT, THESE, THIS, MY, AND NO ARE NOUN SIGNALS. ALMOST EVERY TIME YOU SEE ONE, YOU KNOW A NOUN WILL FOLLOW.

EXAMPLES: Those dishes
Our house

Circle each noun signal in the sentences below. Underline each noun.

1.   The dog wagged its tail.

2.   My brother went to the movie.

3.   Every student must study for the test.

4.   The man takes the bus each day.

5.   Your bike has a flat tire.

6.   These eggs are rotten.

7.   This apple is green.

8.   No dogs are allowed in the library.

9.   Each player has a uniform.

10. The family painted their house.

List 12 nouns you have underlined.   **List 12 noun signals you have circled.**

NOUNS   **NOUN SIGNALS**

_____ _____   _____ _____
_____ _____   _____ _____
_____ _____   _____ _____
_____ _____   _____ _____
_____ _____   _____ _____
_____ _____   _____ _____

On a separate sheet of paper, write 5 sentences. Use _an_ in each sentence.

NOUNS

COMMON AND PROPER

> A NOUN THAT NAMES <u>ANY</u> PERSON, PLACE, OR THING IS CALLED A <u>COMMON</u> <u>NOUN</u>.
>
> EXAMPLES: girl school dog
>
> A NOUN THAT NAMES A <u>PARTICULAR</u> OR A <u>SPECIAL</u> PERSON, PLACE, OR THING IS CALLED A <u>PROPER</u> <u>NOUN</u>. CAPITALIZE NOUNS WHICH ARE PARTICULAR OR SPECIAL, SUCH AS INDIVIDUAL PERSONS, NAMED PLACES, LABELED THINGS.
>
> EXAMPLES: David Phoenix Chevrolet

Fill in each blank with a proper noun.

1. My school's name is _____.

2. My cousin's name is _____.

3. If I could buy a car, it would be a _____.

4. My favorite song is _____.

5. The capital of my state is _____.

6. My favorite movie was _____.

7. My teacher's name is _____.

Fill in each blank with a common noun.

1. Last week, I bought a _____.

2. Once, I lost my _____.

3. Yesterday, I went to the _____.

4. We took a _____ on our camping trip.

5. We saw a _____ at the zoo.

6. I found a _____.

On a separate sheet of paper, write 6 sentences. Use a proper noun in each sentence.

NOUNS

MORE THAN ONE WORD

> **SOME NOUNS ARE MADE UP OF MORE THAN ONE WORD.**
> **EXAMPLES:**   Atlantic Ocean   sister-in-law

In the following sentences, underline all the nouns of more than one word.

1.   Uncle Robert joined the police force.

2.   When we visited San Francisco, we saw the Golden Gate Bridge.

3.   Mrs. Grady deposited her money in the Valley National Bank.

4.   My mother-in-law owns the Golden Crust Bakery.

5.   We saw Ronald McDonald at Legend City Park.

6.   The Saint Bernard is famous for rescuing lost travelers.

7.   The lowest and hottest spot in the United States is Death Valley.

8.   The Fourth of July is usually a very warm day.

9.   Judy played ping-pong with Aunt Ellen.

10.   Cousin George works at the post office.

11.   My father-in-law works for the fire department.

12.   Stan Smith has an office in the Chrysler Building.

13.   The Maricopa Freeway passes through Phoenix, Arizona.

You have underlined nouns of more than one word. On a separate sheet of paper, list 5 other nouns that appear in the sentences.

NOUNS

COMMON AND PROPER

For each common noun below, write a proper noun.
Remember, a proper noun must begin with a capital letter.

1. city _____
2. state _____
3. school _____
4. continent _____
5. book _____

6. month _____
7. ocean _____
8. street _____
9. country _____
10. newspaper _____

For each proper noun below, write a common noun.

1. Europe _____
2. Italy _____
3. Iowa _____
4. Memphis _____
5. Halloween _____

6. Abraham Lincoln _____
7. Chevrolet _____
8. Star Wars _____
9. Black Beauty _____
10. Jingle Bells _____

Fill in each blank with a proper noun.

1. _____ barked at the stranger.

2. My cat's name is _____.

3. My grandfather owns a _____.

4. My favorite movie is _____.

On a separate sheet of paper, list 6 proper nouns that name things that would be found in your city.

NOUNS

COMMON AND PROPER

The nouns in the sentences have been underlined.
If the noun is common, write C above it.
If the noun is proper, write P above it.

1. I have an <u>account</u> at the <u>united</u> <u>bank</u>.

2. <u>Tony</u> drove his new <u>car</u> to <u>florida</u>.

3. The <u>french</u> make delicious <u>bread</u>.

4. I bought <u>shoes</u> at <u>bullock's</u> <u>department</u> <u>store</u>.

5. While in <u>new york</u>, we'll visit <u>the</u> <u>empire</u> <u>state</u> <u>building</u>.

6. My <u>teacher</u> read a <u>book</u> called <u>the</u> <u>secret</u> <u>garden</u>.

7. A new <u>bridge</u> will be built across the <u>salt</u> <u>river</u>.

8. In <u>april</u>, we will move to <u>tucson</u>.

9. In <u>england</u>, <u>elevators</u> are called <u>lifts</u>.

10. The <u>papago</u> <u>indians</u> live in <u>arizona</u>.

11. Did you see <u>mrs.</u> <u>smith</u>, our <u>teacher</u>?

12. My <u>aunt</u> knew the famous <u>actor</u>, <u>clark</u> <u>gable</u>.

13. I think <u>sandra's</u> <u>birthday</u> is in <u>january</u>.

14. Many <u>indians</u> live in <u>arizona</u>.

15. The <u>family</u> moved from <u>cleveland</u> to <u>memphis</u>.

On a separate sheet of paper, write all the nouns you have marked P. Be sure to capitalize.

NOUNS

PROPER

The proper nouns in each sentence have not been capitalized.
Rewrite each sentence. Capitalize the proper nouns.

1. The browns visited the grand canyon in may. _____

   _____

2. The pima indians live on a reservation in arizona. _____

   _____

3. When we were in paris, we visited the eiffel tower. _____

   _____

4. The nile river flows through egypt. _____

   _____

5. aunt millie and uncle max were married in june. _____

   _____

6. The dutch first settled in new york. _____

   _____

7. Many mexicans have moved to california and texas. _____

   _____

8. The indianapolis 500 takes place every memorial day. _____

   _____

Select an article from a newspaper or magazine. Circle six proper nouns.

NOUNS

COMMON AND PROPER

REVIEW

Write a proper noun suggested by each of these common nouns.

1. school _____
2. teacher _____
3. friend _____
4. day _____

5. state _____
6. car _____
7. dog _____
8. city _____

Write a common noun suggested by each of these proper nouns.

1. Linda _____
2. James _____
3. Monday _____
4. Ohio _____
5. Europe _____

6. Italy _____
7. March _____
8. Denver _____
9. Christmas _____
10. Mrs. Brown _____

Circle each common noun and underline each proper noun.

1. The giant tortoise of the Galapagos Islands is an animal that lives a long life.

2. Oregon produces more lumber than any other state in the nation.

3. Many deer, elk, and antelope can be found in the fields and forests of Oregon.

4. The King Ranch in Texas is about the size of the state of Rhode Island.

5. Many people in Kentucky live in small towns or on farms.

On a separate sheet of paper, write six sentences. Use a proper noun in each sentence.

NOUNS

SINGULAR AND PLURAL

WHEN A NOUN REFERS TO <u>ONE</u> THING, THE NOUN IS <u>SINGULAR</u>.

EXAMPLES: A bird   The house

WHEN A NOUN REFERS TO <u>MORE THAN ONE</u> THING, THE NOUN IS <u>PLURAL</u>.

EXAMPLES: Two birds   Three houses

Write S in the blank if the noun is singular. Write P in the blank if the noun is plural.

pie	_____	hot dogs	_____	carrots	_____
cakes	_____	apple	_____	banana	_____
cookies	_____	taco	_____	oranges	_____
hamburger	_____	potatoes	_____	lemons	_____

Circle the plural nouns.

1.   The driver hit both cars.
2.   My sisters like puppies and kittens.
3.   The teachers and students ate lunch.
4.   We saw an elephant and some camels at the zoo.
5.   Put the eggs in the refrigerator.
6.   The houses near the tracks were torn down.
7.   The rain ruined the books.
8.   The clouds blocked the sun.
9.   The girls each ate two hamburgers.

1.   **Select a newspaper article, magazine article, or pages in a book.**
2.   **Find ten plural nouns and ten singular nouns.**
3.   **On a separate sheet of paper, list the plural nouns and the singular nouns you have found.**

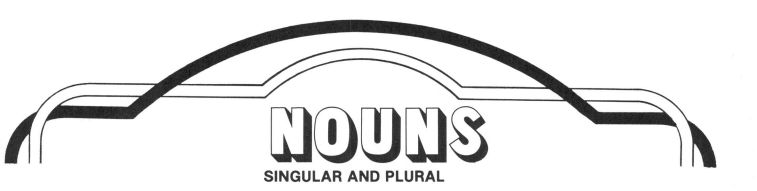

NOUNS

SINGULAR AND PLURAL

MANY NOUNS FORM THE PLURAL BY JUST ADDING <u>S</u> TO THE SINGULAR NOUNS.

EXAMPLES: dog   dogs
            horse   horses

TO FORM THE PLURAL OF A NOUN ENDING IN <u>S</u>, <u>X</u>, <u>Z</u>, <u>SH</u>, OR <u>CH</u>, ADD <u>ES</u>.

EXAMPLE: fox   foxes

Write the plurals.

tree _____	shoe _____	bicycle _____
school _____	boat _____	skate _____
week _____	table _____	truck _____
hotel _____	animal _____	coat _____

Write the plurals.

bush _____	switch _____	buzz _____
wish _____	peach _____	waltz _____
box _____	watch _____	glass _____
tax _____	pass _____	match _____

Write the plurals.

class _____	patch _____
bench _____	pizza _____
brush _____	dress _____
train _____	wax _____
newspaper _____	magazine _____

On a separate sheet of paper, write a different sentence using the plural form of each of these nouns: fox, ax, blanket, ranch, ring, wish, speech.

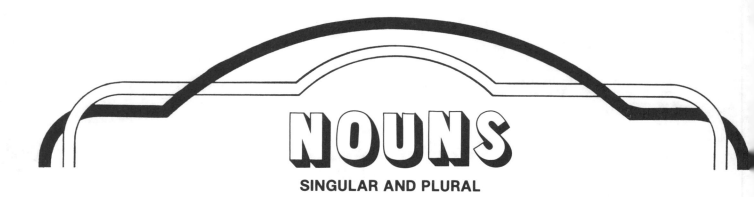

NOUNS

SINGULAR AND PLURAL

> When a singular noun ends in y with a consonant before it,
> change the y to i and add es.
>
> Example: pansy   pansies
>
> When a singular noun ends in y with a vowel before it, add s.
>
> Example: monkey   monkeys

Write the plurals.

country _____	alley _____	ray _____
monkey _____	baby _____	county _____
candy _____	pony _____	toy _____
key _____	guy _____	penny _____
family _____	joy _____	boy _____
valley _____	day _____	story _____
pantry _____	dummy _____	donkey _____
sky _____	way _____	lady _____
memory _____	factory _____	play _____
tray _____	party _____	city _____

**On a separate sheet of paper, use the plural form of each of these nouns in a different
sentence:** journey, delay, secretary, nursery, opportunity, holiday.

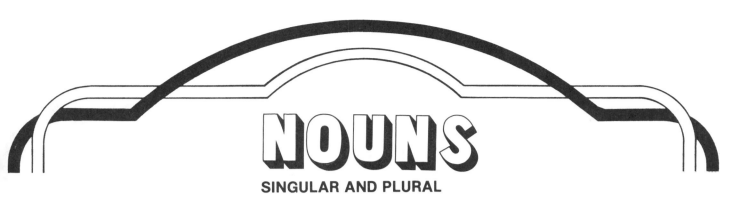

NOUNS

SINGULAR AND PLURAL

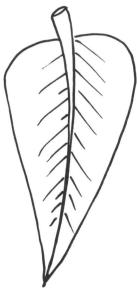

MANY NOUNS ENDING IN <u>O</u> ADD <u>S</u> TO FORM THE PLURAL. THIS INCLUDES NOUNS ENDING IN <u>O</u> PRECEDED BY A VOWEL, AND ALL MUSICAL TERMS.

EXAMPLE: piano   pianos

SOME NOUNS THAT END WITH <u>O</u> ADD <u>ES</u> TO FORM THE PLURAL.

EXAMPLE: tomato   tomatoes

MANY NOUNS ENDING IN <u>F</u> OR <u>FE</u> CHANGE THE <u>F</u> OR <u>FE</u> TO <u>VE</u> AND ADD <u>S</u>, BUT SOME SIMPLY ADD <u>S</u>.

EXAMPLE: calf   calves
chief   chiefs

Write the plurals. Use a dictionary if necessary.

patio	_____	ditto	_____	self	_____
potato	_____	calf	_____	zoo	_____
studio	_____	wolf	_____	leaf	_____
knife	_____	roof	_____	dwarf	_____
chef	_____	tomato	_____	elf	_____
motto	_____	zero	_____	burro	_____
volcano	_____	wharf	_____	life	_____
hero	_____	thief	_____	rodeo	_____
wife	_____	half	_____	chief	_____
solo	_____	shelf	_____	igloo	_____
banjo	_____	loaf	_____	bongo	_____

On a separate sheet of paper, write a different sentence using the plural form of each of these nouns: knife, echo, wolf, leaf, banjo, potato.

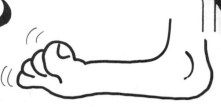

NOUNS

SINGULAR AND PLURAL

**CONSTANT FORM AND
MAJOR SPELLING CHANGES**

SOME NOUNS FORM THEIR PLURAL WITH <u>IRREGULAR</u> <u>ENDINGS</u>.

EXAMPLE: child   children

SOME NOUNS <u>CHANGE</u> <u>LETTERS</u> WITHIN THE WORD.

EXAMPLE: tooth   teeth

SOME NOUNS <u>DO</u> <u>NOT</u> <u>CHANGE</u> FORM FOR PLURALS.

EXAMPLE: deer   deer

Use a dictionary to find the plural form for each of the following nouns.

1. ox _____
2. goose _____
3. sheep _____
4. foot _____
5. man _____
6. fish _____
7. moose _____
8. reindeer _____
9. louse _____

10. woman _____
11. child _____
12. buffalo _____
13. elk _____
14. chairman _____
15. mouse _____
16. swine _____
17. salesman _____
18. series _____

Each noun in parentheses is singular. Write a sentence using the plural form.

1. (tooth) _____
2. (goose) _____
3. (deer) _____
4. (ox) _____
5. (sheep) _____
6. (woman) _____

NOUNS

CONSTANT FORM

AND MAJOR SPELLING CHANGES

In each sentence, write the plural form of the noun printed in parentheses.

1. Several _____ were playing in the park. (child)

2. We spotted a herd of _____ in the valley. (deer)

3. A team of strong _____ pulled the wagon. (ox)

4. A gaggle of _____ crossed the road. (goose)

5. The hunter shot two _____. (elk)

6. How many _____ did you catch? (fish)

7. The _____ will meet tomorrow. (chairman)

8. We saw several _____ at the zoo. (reindeer)

9. There were three _____ in the store. (woman)

10. The dirty animal was covered with _____. (louse)

11. The boy had large _____. (foot)

12. There were two _____ in the store. (salesman)

13. The little girl's front _____ were missing. (tooth)

14. We caught some _____ in our traps. (mouse)

On a separate sheet of paper, use the plural form of each of these nouns in a different sentence: moose, woman, dormouse, deer, swine.

NOUNS

SINGULAR AND PLURAL

Rewrite these sentences making each underlined noun plural. It will be necessary to make certain other changes so that the sentence will be correct.

    EXAMPLE: This hamburger would be better with a sliced tomato.
                        The hamburgers would be better with sliced tomatoes.

1.   The <u>monkey</u> picked a <u>leaf</u> from the <u>tree</u>. _____

    _____

2.   The <u>wolf</u> and the <u>donkey</u> ran away. _____

    _____

3.   The <u>man</u> had to defend his <u>belief</u>. _____

    _____

4.   The <u>child</u> listened for the <u>echo</u> in the canyon. _____

    _____

5.   The <u>hero</u> returned with the <u>chief</u>. _____

    _____

6.   I threw the <u>sandwich</u> into the <u>bush</u>. _____

    _____

7.   The <u>factory</u> closed for the <u>holiday</u>. _____

    _____

8.   Put the <u>key</u> and the <u>knife</u> on the <u>shelf</u>. _____

    _____

On a separate sheet of paper, write a different sentence using the plural form of each of these nouns: shelf, hobo, domino, mouse, foot, piano, life, calf.

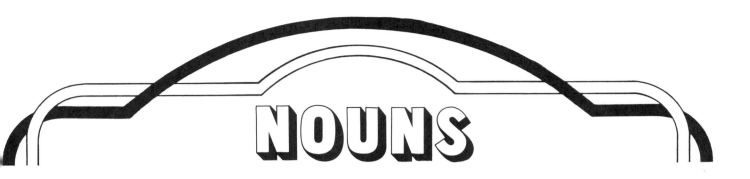

NOUNS

REVIEW

Write the plural form for the following nouns.

1.	driver	_____	14.	rose bush	_____
2.	lunch	_____	15.	convoy	_____
3.	city	_____	16.	secretary	_____
4.	quarter	_____	17.	sheep	_____
5.	deer	_____	18.	tooth	_____
6.	wolf	_____	19.	tax	_____
7.	journey	_____	20.	mouse	_____
8.	rash	_____	21.	ability	_____
9.	self	_____	22.	knife	_____
10.	pencil	_____	23.	clock	_____
11.	survey	_____	24.	duty	_____
12.	half	_____	25.	ranch	_____
13.	dwarf	_____	26.	gulf	_____

On a separate sheet of paper, use the plural of each of these nouns in a different sentence: thief, moose, elf, country, peach, child, goose, turkey, opportunity, wish.

NOUNS

SINGULAR AND PLURAL

REVIEW

Write the plural form of each noun in the blank above it.

1. The _____ came from several _____.
   family   country

2. They traveled over _____ and through _____.
   mountain   valley

3. The _____ served _____,
   wife   turkey

   _____, and _____.
   potato   vegetable

4. The _____ picked _____,
   child   strawberry

   _____, and _____.
   blueberry   cherry

5. The man brought his _____, _____,
   monkey   donkey

   and _____.
   pony

6. Two _____ holding _____ watched two
   lady   baby

   _____ steal ten _____ of bread from the
   man   loaf

   _____.
   shelf

7. The _____ quickly called two _____.
   woman   policeman

8. The _____ ran through several _____
   officer   alley

   before they caught the _____.
   thief

On a separate sheet of paper, write a paragraph using the following nouns: houses, trees, sun, clouds, sky, weather, storm, rain, lightning, thunder, damage. **Underline all the nouns in the paragraph.**

NOUNS

POSSESSIVE - SINGULAR

POSSESSIVES SHOW THAT SOMETHING IS OWNED. SINGULAR NOUNS SHOW POSSESSION WITH AN APOSTROPHE AND S.

EXAMPLES: student's book
family's car

Possessives replace the words belonging to. Simplify the groups of words by using possessive nouns. Write the new phrase on the line.

Car belonging to Tom _____

Horse belonging to Spike _____

Bicycle belonging to Nick _____

Football belonging to Roger _____

Record belonging to Dave _____

Bottle belonging to a baby _____

Coat belonging to Clyde _____

Shirt belonging to Sheldon _____

Tube belonging to Tim _____

House belonging to Harvey _____

Hat belonging to Hilda _____

Ring belonging to Rhonda _____

Chain belonging to Cheri _____

1. **On a separate sheet of paper, write the singular possessive of each noun below. Add a noun signal and a word to name what is possessed.**

    EXAMPLE: sister   My sister's boyfriend

    teacher, friend, mother, brother, dog, cat, cowboy

2. **Use each of the above groups of words in a sentence.**

    EXAMPLE: My sister's boyfriend called.

27

NOUNS

POSSESSIVE - PLURAL

> Possessives show that something is owned.
> Plural nouns ending in <u>S</u> show possession with an <u>apostrophe</u> only.
>
>   **EXAMPLE:**   students' books   families' cars
>
> Plural nouns not ending in <u>S</u> show possession with an <u>apostrophe</u> and <u>S</u>.
>
>   **EXAMPLES:**   men's coat   mice's cheese

Possessives replace the words <u>belonging to</u>. Simplify these groups of words by using possessive nouns. Write the new phrase in the blank.

Desks belonging to the teachers   _____

Tractors belonging to the farmers   _____

Tails belonging to the mice   _____

Shoes belonging to the children   _____

Badges belonging to the policemen   _____

Bones belonging to the dogs   _____

Paws belonging to the cats   _____

Feathers belonging to the geese   _____

Yokes belonging to the oxen   _____

Poles belonging to the fishermen   _____

Office belonging to the doctors   _____

Chairs belonging to the pupils   _____

On a separate sheet of paper, write the plural possessive of each noun below. Use each word in a different sentence.

monkey, baby, woman, sheep, deer, family, hero, wife

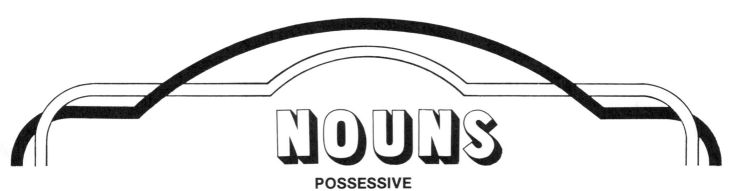

NOUNS

POSSESSIVE

SINGULAR AND PLURAL

Fill in each blank with the possessive form of the word in parentheses.

1. the _____ ship (captain)

2. the _____ duties (sailors)

3. the _____ camp (Indians)

4. the _____ office (doctor)

5. the _____ waiting room (dentists)

6. the _____ paddles (canoes)

7. the _____ gun (hunter)

8. the _____ tail (fox)

9. the _____ fins (shark)

10. the _____ plot (movie)

11. the _____ hats (gentlemen)

12. the _____ stems (daisies)

13. the _____ tires (tricycle)

14. the _____ nest (mice)

On a separate sheet of paper, use each of these possessive nouns in a different sentence.
teacher's, teachers'   student's, students'

NOUNS

POSSESSIVE

SINGULAR AND PLURAL

Fill in each blank with the possessive form of the word in parentheses.

1. (car)   The _____ fender was smashed.

2. (aunts)   All my _____ children are boys.

3. (soldiers)   The _____ uniforms were blue.

4. (seal)   One of the _____ enemies is the shark.

5. (porcupines)   The _____ young are born in late May.

6. (witches)   The _____ hats were black.

7. (firemen)   We saw the _____ truck speed away.

8. (tailors)   I couldn't find the _____ shop.

9. (clock)   The _____ hands stopped at 8:30.

10. (train)   We heard the _____ whistle.

11. (students)   The _____ books were stolen.

12. (deer)   The hunter mounted the _____ antlers.

13. (donkeys)   The _____ braying scared the child.

14. (storm)   A small plane flew near the _____ eye.

On a separate sheet of paper, write the singular and plural possessive of each noun below. Add a noun signal and a word to name what is possessed.

> **EXAMPLE: boy boy's   The boy's bike. (singular)**
>
> **boys'   The boys' bikes (plural)**
>
> horse, elephant, child, mouse, man, fox

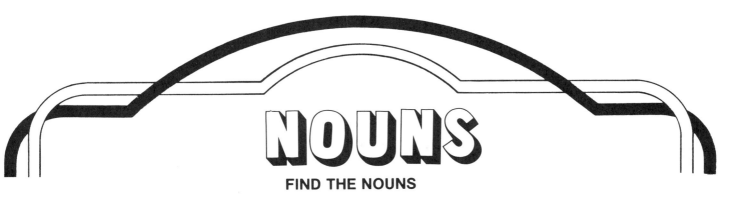

NOUNS

FIND THE NOUNS

Look for nouns in the picture below.

Write 8 common nouns.

_____ _____

_____ _____

_____ _____

_____ _____

Write 4 nouns that show possession.

_____ _____

_____ _____

Write 4 proper nouns.

_____ _____

_____ _____

Write 4 plural nouns.

_____ _____

_____ _____

_____ _____

FASHION SQUARE MALL

PRONOUNS

RECOGNITION

A PRONOUN IS A WORD THAT TAKES THE PLACE OF A NOUN.

Example: Bonnie says <u>she</u> likes tennis.
(The pronoun <u>she</u> stands for Bonnie.)

Some common pronouns are:

I, me, my, mine, you, your, yours, he, his, him, she, her, hers, our, ours, we, us, it, its, they, their, theirs, and them

Underline the pronouns in the following sentences.

1.   I lost my books.

2.   Please give me your phone number.

3.   Is the package yours or mine?

4.   She said he found her address.

5.   Our new house is on your street.

6.   The children said their parents would take them home.

7.   Your puppy is wagging its tail.

8.   My brother wants his car waxed.

9.   We threw the ball to him, and he caught it.

10.   He told me you had finished your work.

11.   Her bicycle was destroyed when she ran over it.

12.   Would you like to help my brother and me?

13.   The wind hit them in their faces as they skied down the mountain.

14.   The book on her desk is mine.

On a separate sheet of paper, write 6 sentences. Use a different pronoun in each sentence.

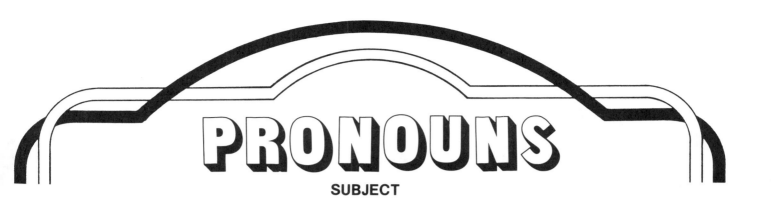

PRONOUNS

SUBJECT

The words <u>I</u>, <u>you</u>, <u>he</u>, <u>she</u>, <u>it</u>, <u>we</u>, and <u>they</u> are <u>subject</u> <u>pronouns</u>.

Rewrite each sentence, replacing the underlined word or phrase with the correct pronoun.
EXAMPLE: the <u>girl</u> fell. She fell.

1.   The <u>boy</u> ran. _____

2.   <u>Mary</u> was late. _____

3.   The <u>truck</u> is blue. _____

4.   <u>Mrs. White</u> yelled. _____

5.   <u>Mrs. Ray</u> worked. _____

6.   <u>Joey</u> frowned. _____

7.   <u>Tom</u> and <u>I</u> jogged. _____

8.   The <u>bug</u> crawled. _____

9.   <u>Jake</u> went swimming. _____

10.   <u>Mr. and Mrs. Green</u> live here. _____

11.   My <u>mother</u> and <u>I</u> cleaned house. _____

12.   My <u>teeth</u> are clean. _____

On a separate sheet of paper, use each of the following pronouns in a different sentence:
I, you, he, she, it, we, and they.

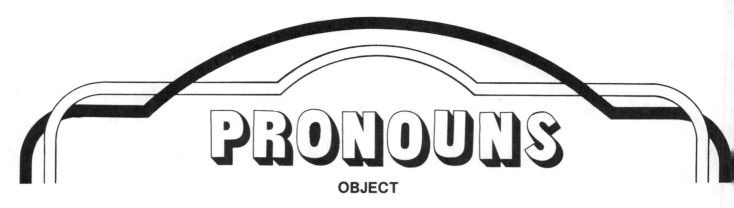

PRONOUNS

OBJECT

The words <u>me</u>, <u>you</u>, <u>him</u>, <u>her</u>, <u>it</u>, <u>us</u>, and <u>them</u> are object pronouns.

Rewrite each sentence, replacing the underlined word or phrase with the correct pronoun.
EXAMPLE: He likes <u>Jane</u>. He likes her.

1.   Give the book to <u>Ed</u>. _____

2.   Paul saw <u>Ted and Alice</u>. _____

3.   I don't like <u>spinach</u>. _____

4.   A dog chased <u>my brother and me</u>. _____

5.   She painted <u>her room</u> yellow. _____

6.   With <u>the mother cat</u> were two kittens. _____

   _____

7.   This car belongs to <u>Mr. Ong</u>. _____

8.   The teacher likes <u>Lynn and me</u>. _____

9.   My friend gave <u>my sister</u> a ride. _____

   _____

10. The food looked good to <u>Sondra</u>. _____

   _____

On a separate sheet of paper, use each of the following pronouns in a different sentence:
you, him, her, it, us, and them.

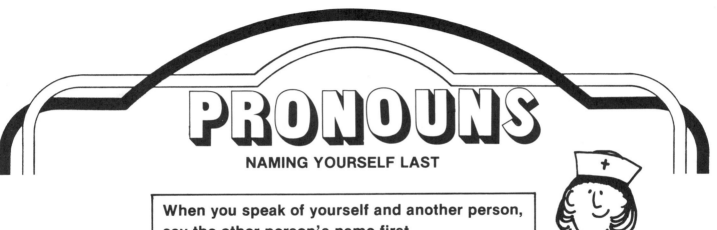

PRONOUNS

NAMING YOURSELF LAST

When you speak of yourself and another person, say the other person's name first.

Underline the correct form in parentheses. Write a sentence leaving out the incorrect form.

    EXAMPLE: (<u>Jody and I</u>, I and Jody) went fishing.   **Jody and I went fishing.**

1.   (My brother and I, I and my brother) bought new bicycles. _____

_____

2.   The coach gave uniforms to (me and Jed, Jed and me). _____

_____

3.   (Gina and I, I and Gina) want to be nurses. _____

_____

4.   The huge dog barked at (my dad and me, me and my dad). _____

_____

5.   (I and Archie, Archie and I) camped by the lake. _____

_____

6.   A car nearly hit (me and my brother, my brother and me). _____

_____

7.   (Julie and I, I and Julie) will go to the store. _____

_____

On a separate sheet of paper, use each of the following phrases in a different sentence:
Mother and I, My friend and I, Lisa and I, John and I.

PRONOUNS

POSSESSIVE

> Possessive pronouns take the place of nouns that show ownership.
> The possessive forms of pronouns are these:
>
> my, mine   our, ours   your, yours
>
> his, her, hers, its   their, theirs

Rewrite the sentence, replacing the word or phrase in parentheses with the correct possessive pronoun.

EXAMPLE: The white cat is (Virginia's).   **The white cat is hers.**

1. The dog licked (the dog's) tail.

   _____

2. The children are saving (the children's) money.

   _____

3. The blue coat is (Lisa's).

   _____

4. The chocolate ice cream is (Wendy's and mine).

   _____

5. Tonya curled (Tonya's) hair.

   _____

6. The bird injured (the bird's) wing.

   _____

7. Jim washed (Jim's) car.

   _____

On a separate sheet of paper, write five sentences using one of the following pronouns in each sentence: my, your, our, its, their

PRONOUNS

POSSESSIVE

Circle each possessive pronoun in the sentences below.

1. Did your cat hurt its paw?

2. Our family enjoyed your performance.

3. My brother is taller than his teacher.

4. My cousins enjoyed their vacation.

5. His horse lost its shoe.

6. If your car won't start, take ours.

7. Is that car theirs?

8. The blue coat is mine.

9. The horse broke its leg.

10. Have you taken your turn?

11. Our new car is in the garage.

12. My aunt lost her keys.

13. This room is yours.

14. The teacher was happy with his class.

15. Is this our bus?

16. Your puppy lost its collar.

17. Most of that mess is mine.

18. Our team won its game.

19. His best friend is my cousin.

20. Your cat likes its new toy.

On a separate sheet of paper, write four sentences using one of the following pronouns in each sentence: mine, ours, theirs, yours

PRONOUNS

I AND ME

To know whether to use I or me in a sentence such as, "Bob and (I, me) went shopping," leave out "Bob and." It is correct to say, "I went shopping." You would not say, "Me went shopping." Therefore, it is correct to say, "Bob and I went shopping."

In a sentence such as, "Give the books to Bob and (I, me)," leave out "Bob and." It is correct to say, "Give the books to me." You would not say, "Give the books to I." Therefore, it is correct to say, "Give the books to Bob and me."

Underline the correct pronoun in parentheses. Rewrite each sentence, leaving out the incorrect pronoun.

   Example: Mac and (me, I) walked home.   Mac and I walked home.

1.   Ron and (me, I) had to stay after school.

   _____

2.   Mr. Sims gave some flowers to Diane and (I, me).

   _____

3.   Phil and (me, I) have skateboards.

   _____

4.   Mother bought lunch for Jeff and (I, me).

   _____

5.   Rachel and (me, I) like horses.

   _____

6.   The pizza is all for you and (me, I).

   _____

7.   You and (me, I) can go outside now.

   _____

PRONOUNS

I AND ME

Write I or me in each blank.

1. Were you looking for Debbie and _____?

2. You and _____ can walk home together.

3. My father and _____ played catch.

4. May Rick and _____ have a ride?

5. Is there any work for you and _____?

6. The dog growled at Victor and _____.

7. The cookies are for either you or _____.

8. My mother and _____ will take you home.

9. Would you like Art and _____ to help you?

10. My cousin played a trick on my sister and _____.

11. Miss Stevens and _____ are invited to a party.

12. My dog and _____ are pals.

13. The teacher gave an award to Randy and _____.

14. The principal told Mike and _____ to go to class.

15. The tennis balls belong to my brother and _____.

16. Mom dropped Jeff and _____ off at the library.

17. Kim and _____ wrote the story.

On a separate sheet of paper, write 4 sentences. Use one of the following pronouns in each sentence: I, me

39

PRONOUNS

REVIEW

Rewrite the following sentences. Substitute a pronoun for the underlined word or words.
EXAMPLE: Bob has finished <u>Bob's</u> work.
Bob has finished his work.

1. Joan lost <u>Joan's</u> keys.

_____

2. Dad washed <u>dad's</u> car.

_____

3. Kenny tied <u>Kenny's</u> shoe.

_____

4. Please throw the ball to <u>Jim</u>.

_____

5. <u>Steve and Lisa</u> went home.

_____

6. The records belong to <u>Julie and Robyn</u>.

_____

7. The puppy wagged <u>the puppy's</u> tail.

_____

8. Jan wanted us to write to <u>Jan</u>.

_____

9. <u>A bug</u> crawled across the table.

_____

On a separate sheet of paper, write six sentences. Use one of the following pronouns in each sentence: their, them, his, her, they, and we.

REVIEW

1. **Write nouns that name persons, places, or things.**

    PERSONS   PLACES   THINGS

    _____   _____   _____

    _____   _____   _____

    _____   _____   _____

2. **Circle nouns in the sentences.**

    Dogs can be used to guard houses and stores. During wars, dogs helped find

    wounded soldiers and also carried messages.

    Children of long ago had many unusual toys. They played with sticks, twigs,

    cones, rocks, and shells.

3. **Underline nouns you can see, touch, smell, or hear.**
    Circle nouns that name a feeling or an idea.

    The man said, "I wish you health and happiness."

    The mother felt pride and love as she looked at her child.

    The teacher had high hopes for her students.

4. **Circle each noun signal in these sentences.**

    The woman bought a chair at an antique shop.

    Each dog stood by its owner.

    Those boxes contain the extra books.

    Every student received an award.

41

REVIEW

5. **Circle all nouns of more than one word.**

A sea mouse isn't a mouse that lives in the sea.

People who live in Nova Scotia are called Bluenoses.

The fourth Saturday of September is called Kid's Day.

6. **Circle each common noun. Underline each proper noun.**

The Chinese celebrate New Year's for 15 days.

On June 11, 1897, Solomon Andree and his companion attempted to fly over the

North Pole in a balloon.

Charles A. Lindbergh's nonstop flight from New York to Paris in 1927 covered

3,610 miles.

7. **Circle the pronouns in the following sentences.**

She bakes cookies for her children. They like them. Their voices say, "Thank you."

8. **In the blank, write the pronoun that can replace the word or phrase in parentheses.**

(Henry and I) watched the planes land.   _____

(The little girl) dropped her purse.   _____

Hold the rope for (Chris and me).   _____

The party is for (Steve).   _____

9. **Write the plural of each noun.**

lunch _____ leaf _____ child _____

chief _____ cherry _____ monkey _____

apple _____ tooth _____ tax _____

REVIEW

10. Fill in each blank with the possessive of the word in parentheses.

_____ car has a flat tire. (David)

The _____ coats were in the closet. (ladies)

The _____ trip was a success. (salesmen)

The _____ uniforms were new. (nurses)

11. Underline the correct form in parentheses.

(Martin and I, I and Martin) had a long talk.

All the girls stared at (Phil and me, me and Phil).

(Rosie and I, I and Rosie) played tennis.

Lois took a picture of (Clark and me, me and Clark).

12. Write the correct possessive pronoun in the blank.

The puppy ate _____ food.
              (the puppy's)

Tom and Lisa bought _____ bikes at Bike World.
                             (Tom and Lisa's)

_____ bike is blue.
     (Tom's)

_____ bike is red.
     (Lisa's)

13. Cross out the incorrect word.

Frank and (I, me) went to the library.

Give the flowers to Alice and (me, I).

Write a letter to Eddie and (I, me).

Barbara and (I, me) finished our work.

43

NOUNS

A noun is a word used to name a person, place, or thing.

COMMON AND PROPER

A noun that names any person, place, or thing is called a common noun.

Examples: girl   school   dog

A noun that names a particular or a special person, place, or thing is called a proper noun. Capitalize nouns which are particular or special, such as individual persons, named places, labeled things.

Examples: David   Phoenix   Chevrolet

SINGULAR AND PLURAL

When a noun refers to one thing, the noun is singular.   Example: A bird

When a noun refers to more than one thing, the noun is plural.   Example: Two birds

Many nouns form the plural by just adding s to the singular noun.

Example: dog   dogs

To form the plural of a noun ending in s, x, z, sh, or ch, add es.   Example: fox   foxes

To form the plural of a noun ending in a consonant which comes before y, change y to i and add es.   Example: story   stories

Many nouns ending in o add s to form the plural. This includes nouns ending in o preceded by a vowel and all musical terms.

Examples: zoo   zoos   piano   pianos

Some nouns that end with o add es to form the plural.

Example: potato   potatoes

Many nouns ending in f or fe change the f or fe to ve and add s, but some simply add s.

Example: leaf   leaves   chief   chiefs

Some nouns form their plural with irregular endings.

Example: child   children

Some nouns change letters within a word.

Example: tooth   teeth

Some nouns do not change form for plurals.

Example: deer   deer

POSSESSIVE

Singular nouns show possession with an apostrophe and s.

Example: boy's hat

Plural nouns ending in s show possession with an apostrophe only.   Example: boys' hats

Plural nouns not ending in s show possession with an apostrophe and s.

Example: men's coats